On The Other Side
Of Disappointment

On The OTHER SIDE Of DISAPPOINTMENT

How to re-engage in life after major setbacks and disappointments

RICK BREWSTER

Xulon Press
2301 Lucien Way #415
Maitland, FL 32751
407.339.4217
www.xulonpress.com

Printed in the United States of America.

ISBN-13: 978-1-54565-136-0

TABLE OF CONTENTS

PREFACE

I was asked how long it has taken me to write this book; my reply was, "*About forty years*." The backstory is that the first half of life was pretty amazing. My family and I progressed through life and career without many glitches, and all were happy. Our family consisted of my wife and I, and our two children. We had lots of good friends, enjoyed what we did and where we lived in both Canada and the United States.

I was employed with a church denomination, serving in several roles. Within a few years, we were presented with a wonderful opportunity to live and minister in Asia and, later, Australia. Raising our children in multicultural environments provided them with a great worldview. Life overseas was lots of fun.

When a promotion was offered to move to the international office, I saw this as a continued step forward. However, I was ill-prepared for the world of internal politics. Naively, I thought mission was more important than personal agendas, but not so.

Without trying, I found myself embroiled in conflict time and time again. Thirty years with this organization left me with a three-week severance and the beginning of many questions.

Unfortunately, in too many instances, the label "Christian" means little in matters of ethics, fairness, and doing what is right.

Because of my transient, overseas lifestyle of several years, most of my social life revolved around the people I worked with; so losing a career also meant a greatly reduced social calendar. I had no idea how much self-worth and esteem were tied to my work. To say it was a struggle for the next few years would be an understatement.

Five years later, we found ourselves sitting in a doctor's office, hearing the specialist say to my wife, "This disease will take your life." Talk about re-shuffled priorities—I had a crash course on what was truly important in life.

Some months after my wife's funeral, I saw a movie about an astronaut who, due to a freak accident, found herself totally adrift through space all alone. That could have been me. Stop, and pause for a moment; try to imagine the feeling of lost-ness, helplessness, and utter despair. That is how I felt during that time.

It took several years, but in time I met a wonderful woman whose life and career experiences were, unfortunately, very similar to my own. The connection was immediate; God truly brought two lost desert-wanders together to help each other become whole again. To a great degree, she helped me get to the place where I could process what had happened to both of us.

I can now look back over the past few years with perspective. I have examined my heart to be sure I hold no bitterness, but disappointments—well, that is another story. Today, my faith is strong, alive, and, hopefully, a bit wiser. And now, “on the other side of disappointments,” I wanted to leave a few trail clues for others who may also pass this way.

INTRODUCTION

So I sit here today in a better place. A slight breeze blows across my face, gently cooling the morning sun. From the rearview mirror, images over the past several years reveal ominous, dark clouds of stormy weather—not just an isolated shower, but a storm front that brought more than I could have anticipated.

But for now, the storms have passed—at least for a while. Now, on the other side, I can breathe again; peace is settled. Joy is a more frequent emotion than in times past. A new and quiet strength prevails.

The rewind button would not have allowed me to see the storms I was to encounter. The last few years certainly would not have been my ten-year plan. But today, I can say I am a blessed person, a healthier person; although with a few scars to show for the journey.

What you will read in the following pages is not the blow-by-blow report of the battle. Rather, you will read the reflections of one who has been on a journey called life. What I have learned from the journey has provided a few survival skills for me, which I hope to pass along. My prayer is you will find encouragement, and perhaps a tool or two, to assist you, as the journey to the other side of dis-appointment unfolds before you.

Chapter 1
BEWILDERED

Life can bring unwelcome surprises,
so how do you re-engage in life
after going back to zero?

I suspect those whose life has been "perfect," or who have never had significant setbacks, may not relate to this book. But if I may, and I mean no disrespect, I do not relate to them. It is not that I doubt the existence of such people; I just find them to be a rare breed.

I am writing to those whose lives have gone differently than anticipated—those who have had a few left turns, which left them gasping for air; losses which made them feel as if they were teetering on the edge of a cliff, where the slightest whisper of an ill-thought comment could be enough to send them into a free fall. I write to those who have known the staggering bewilderment of wondering what happened, and why.

To put context to this, I come from a background of faith, believing in God's providence and purpose. At times, I have wondered if such a belief has actually compounded my anxiety, when trying to pick up the pieces of my imploded life. Why would a Good Shepherd allow such painful experiences? So, I write to those who are struggling to find a way to re-engage in life after being taken back to zero.

Let's be honest; loss may come to your doorstep dressed in various clothes: loss of a career, of health, of a loved one, of a child, of a marriage, of a dream, etc. You fill in the blanks.

In my experience, the consolation of well-intended friends often left me without consolation. One therapist surmised I needed to connect with nature and find my place in the universe. Not being sure what that meant, I knew it was not the answer I was looking for.

Being a person of faith, I sought the advice of a "Christian" counselor; the conclusion was, "You should read your Bible more." Really? Now, I am not in any way diminishing the power of the Scriptures to shed light on life's most difficult moments, but after many sessions exploring and analyzing my drifting life, this was the best? Next.

The advice of the grief therapist was I should get a dog. Several weeks into that experience, which included a trip to an after-hours emergency pet hospital, breathing treatments for the dog, medications, and a significant bill, I had a BFO (Blinding Flash of the Obvious) moment. The dog was not the answer to my dilemma.

Some say, "Time heals all wounds." While time certainly gives perspective, allowing us to glean much from living with our pain, simply the passage of time is no cure. Time may give us the ability to see the bigger picture and better manage our journey, but to heal devastation? I think not.

You may agree that deep, personal loss leads to feelings of isolation. While we realize the human experience is shared by others, we somehow believe our experiences are unique. The silence of isolation can be deafening. As happens too often, once the initial crisis event is over, other people forget; but you don't. You are left to sort out your life and try to make sense of what has happened. We may try to forget some things, but certain scenes play over and over, etched in our memory banks. We ask, "If others walked this way before us, why didn't they leave us a few helpful clues along the path?"

Let me say this; your journey is unique. While others may have walked similar steps before you, these are *your* steps. And you have every right to feel the pain of disappointments. Just because others have known pain and loss does not diminish what you are experiencing.

You may feel more vulnerable than you have ever been before, but realize a greater level of understanding is within your grasp. Learn to explore all that can be discovered along the path called your *life*.

> *We find that Scripture is most profound in our moments of brokenness.*

The "Christian counselor" may have been closer to the truth than others. The best therapy I have discovered were the moments of solitude, pouring out my heart before God, and letting His word illuminate the prevailing darkness within. We find that Scripture is most profound in our moments of brokenness. When we are willing to let it speak to us, unfiltered, we gain new insight. There, we discover how flawed and shallow our belief systems may have been. When we are willing to let go of what we previously thought, we can embrace a deeper understanding of the Savior who walks with us; who, at times, is the silent partner on this journey.

I am reminded of a poem by Robert Browning Hamilton:

"I walked a mile with pleasure,
she chatted all the way,
leaving me none the wiser
for all she had to say.
I walked a mile with sorrow,
never a word said she.
But oh what I learned from when sorrow,
when sorrow walked with me."[1]

---

[1] Along The Road by Robert Browning Hamilton

Chapter 2
WELCOME TO THE NEW NORMAL

Change happens;
prepared or not,
welcomed or not,
***this is** the new normal.*

Welcome to the new normal. Here, we learn change is a constant. To travel this journey, we need to discard heavy baggage from the past; it will make the trip easier. Navigating the future while holding on to the past is simply exhausting, and frankly impossible. Letting go of the past is not disloyal; it is survival.

So, let me just say, "normal" is overrated. What was normal in previous times certainly is not now. Just take a look at old photos and notice what you were wearing twenty years ago. I rest my case. Try to define "normal"; everybody will have different and personal answers.

Let's get started on this journey of moving forward and leaving the past behind. What I offer here is simply my perspective and my understanding, which I often utilize. Succinctly stated, *this WAS the new normal, and there is no going back to what used to be. Your life has forever changed. It is a waste of energy to try to make the present resemble the past.*

I realize that for many, change can be difficult to embrace. Clearly, change that you initiate is easier to wrap your arms around, but not all change is deliberate and foreseen. Change thrust upon us without our consent can be hard to acknowledge and accept; we resist and resent.

Periodically, the right thing to do is to have a garage sale and clear out clutter. While items may still have value, if you haven't used them in the past six months, it is time to let them go. And sometimes, it is appropriate to jettison, from our lives, things and issues which have become extra baggage on our journey to a new day. Perhaps this is what the writer of the book of Hebrews reveals to us: "Let us throw off ***everything*** that hinders and the sin that ***so easily*** entangles, and let us run with perseverance the race marked out for us."[2]

A couple of truths stand out to me: "***everything***"; so many things in life entangle our feet and distract us from our journeys. These entanglements interfere and consume, leaving us derailed from our purposes. Secondly, notice how **easily** and suddenly we become entangled. You look back and see the tangled mess your life has become and wonder, *How did that happen?*

Life has a tendency to be noisy and distracting. At times, you want to cover your ears and run for cover: looking for solitude, for perspective, for meaning, for truth. You are left trying to discover what is this "race marked out for us." Self-doubt

---

[2] Hebrews 12:1 NIV

can move in, causing you to question actions and motives.

But before we get too far away from the biblical text, let's see one more important truth: it takes perseverance to run this race. For me, that suggests deliberate, intentional choices, which brings me back to the idea of decluttering life. Some things, ideals, and pursuits are just too expensive and do not hold enough value.

It is hard to see an exit from the familiar path for what it is. Well-known and customary aspects of our lives become our support system; the infrastructure with which we surround and insulate ourselves. And when they are taken away, we feel disoriented, confused, and naked. However, we may learn the familiar, to which we have grown accustomed to, may not be the race marked out for us. A deeper, richer understanding of yourself can be discovered in the new normal. So, what was appropriate in the past may not be right for the future.

Losses, as painful as they are, give new lens to scrutinize what we want to hold on to and what we should discard going forward. Living in the new normal requires a lot of adjustments. But take this as permission to let go of entanglements that hold you back.

> *Losses, as painful as they are, give new lens to scrutinize what we want to hold on to and what we should discard going forward.*

Life is a process of sifting and sorting and letting go. Going back to the ancient wisdom of the book of Ecclesiastes, we are told:

> For everything there is a season, and a time for every purpose under heaven: a time to be born, and a time to die; a time to plant, and a time to pluck up that which is planted; a time to kill, and a time to heal; a time to break down, and a time to build up; a time to weep, and a time to laugh; a time to mourn, and a time to dance; a time

> to cast away stones, and a time to gather stones together; a time to embrace, and a time to refrain from embracing; time to seek, and a time to lose; a time to keep, and a time to cast away; a time to rend, and a time to sew; a time to keep silence, and a time to speak; a time to love, and a time to hate; a time for war, and a time for peace.[3]

Many times, when people and things are taken from us, we are not ready to let go. And therein may be the hidden issue: facing the reality that we cannot control much about this life at all. I cannot control what happens; I cannot control other people; I cannot control circumstances. And the brutal truth is, sometimes we cannot even control ourselves; hard lessons for us control freaks.

The Serenity Prayer is aptly named as such:

> God, grant me the serenity
> to accept the things I cannot change;

---

[3] Ecclesiastes 3:1-8 ASV

courage to change the things I can;
and wisdom to know the difference.
Living one day at a time;
Enjoying one moment at a time;
Accepting hardships as the
pathway to peace;
Taking, as He did, this sinful world as it is,
not as I would have it;
Trusting that He will make all things right
if I surrender to His Will;
That I may be reasonably happy in this life
and supremely happy with Him
Forever in the next.[4]

---

[4] The Serenity Prayer is the common name for a prayer written by the American theologian Reinhold Niebuhr according to Wikipedia

Chapter 3

THE ROLE OF DISAPPOINTMENTS

Disappointment realigns priorities.
Misguided thinking blurs focus.

So when the familiar crashes and burns, and you find yourself standing by the wreckage of your life, in total bewilderment, where do you turn? Serenity once known vanishes like a morning mist. In assessing the carnage, we come face to face with how brutal disappointments can be. You had higher hopes of life, bigger expectations of outcomes. We become shocked by the realities of life. So how do you—how *can* you—face disappointments?

May I suggest one of the first toeholds to begin the mountainous ascent? Realize disappointments do not necessarily mean bitterness. Bitterness can be its own entanglement; it is definitely an expensive purchase holding no value.

But disappointments are something else. Can you ever be disappointed with God? The short answer is yes. However, this probably reveals more about our misled expectations rather than God's nature. God does not need anyone's defense; He is God all by Himself. Yet, our shattered expectations demand a response.

John the Baptist confronted his disappointments, asking the question you may have also asked: "Are you the Coming one, or should we wait for someone else?"[5] Jesus concluded His answer with these haunting words: "Blessed is he who is not offended in me."[6] Another translation states it this way, "Blessed is anyone who does not stumble on account of me."[7] I suspect this is not a verse you

---

[5] Matthew 11:3 NIV

[6] Matthew 11:6 NKJV

[7] Matthew 11:6 NIV

have posted on your refrigerator. We question why God would permit events that shake us to our core.

To be honest, this verse troubles me. I wish it wasn't there; without it, the Bible would fit my theology better. But the verse is there, and Jesus Himself said it. And He said it to John at the deepest crisis of his life. So why does God permit adversity, betrayal, and disappointments?

I handle this scripture with great respect. It is not children's Sunday-school theology; this really is one of the big issues of life. Let's face it, sometimes we stumble in life. We stumble when life blindsides us, when Christians disappoint us, with the losses in life. We may be too embarrassed to point a finger of accusation, but in our hearts, we despairingly cry out, "God, why did You let this happen?" As uncomfortable as it may seem, we are stumbling and offended by our disappointments with God.

Again, I say, God does not need my defense. The disappointments which entangle us have more to do with our misled perceptions. We can be misled by our own theology, the emphasis being "our own." The flaw is not in God; it has more to do with our understanding of "the race marked out for us." By the way, I wonder if our theology and God's have much resemblance to each other at all.

Even the best of our theologians have earth-only views. But the scripture reminds us:

> Now we see things imperfectly, like puzzling reflections in a mirror, but then we will see everything with perfect clarity. All that I know now is partial and incomplete, but then I will know everything completely, just as God now knows me completely.[8]

Perhaps we have been misled ever so subtly to think that if we do good, follow God, and live for Him, we will somehow be elevated above losses and disappointments. As much as I would like to believe this, it is a shallow understanding. Again,

---

[8] 1 Corinthians 13:12 NLT

the writer of Hebrews confronts us with one of those awkward, wish-it-wasn't-there scriptures:

> ***All these people were still living by faith when they died.*** They did not receive the things promised; they only saw them and welcomed them from a distance, ***admitting that they were foreigners and strangers on earth***.[9]

This scripture reveals a great truth for us: "admitting that they were foreigners and strangers on earth." Some of life's mysteries will only be fully understood when seen from an eternal perspective. Disappointments can put distorted expectations in a clear focus. We can then realign priorities to what is truly important. The haze of things once embraced as vital pales in the clear light of day.

For those who have walked a mile with sorrow, we tend to process each day differently, treasuring it as a gift. We embrace every day for all its worth

9 Hebrews 12:13 NIV

and learn to be very much present and in the moment. We have been given the gift of realigned priorities. Our eyes begin to recognize new companionship in the fellow sojourners who walk this path with us.

Some may read these words and think I am saying, "Have no expectations, and you will never be disappointed." What a dull, drab, gray world that would be! Let me set the record straight: My understanding of God is that He is more than I could ever imagine. His plans are higher than mine, His ways above mine. God is ever crafting His interventions in our lives to help us let go of shallow monochrome and small perceptions of Him, and dare to embrace a God who is bigger than we understand.

Life can be like the ocean currents washing up on the beach, bringing with it debris and garbage others have carelessly discarded. How easily our steps can be entangled in the backwash. We must constantly untangle the garbage that washes up around us. It trips us, encumbers our stride, and distracts us. It might even put us on a different path—one others have mapped out for us.

God is actively jamming the frequency of messages others have scripted for us. There is a race marked out for us, and God is all about jarring and nudging us to see a higher path. As good and noble as the past may have been, our path to this point has been of a lower altitude than His.

> *"God is actively jamming the frequency of messages others have scripted for us."*

So while the new normal may be hard to embrace, allow me to suggest that a new altitude requires a different intake of oxygen. Rather than breathing the shallow breaths of the exhausted, learn to breathe deeply, filling your lungs with clean, unpolluted air from the new altitude, and breathe out slowly. The new normal altitude is not the smog-filled life of the past with a breathing mask. It is a new altitude.

Have you ever noticed that many athletes train at high altitudes so their lungs can be prepared for their optimum performances? Perhaps what you are facing is preparation for your best performance yet.

Chapter 4
THE STORM

The greatest introductions are often made in the most difficult moments of life.

Let me take you to another passage of scripture; I want you to interject yourself into this story. Oh, wait a minute, perhaps you already have. In Matthew, chapter fourteen an account is given of Jesus and the disciples. Jesus had just performed yet another astounding miracle; I can only imagine the buzz the twelve were feeling—wonder, amazement, courage, gratitude to be a part of something so revolutionary.

Peak moments of our past may resemble those wonderful times the disciples experienced. The words of the psalmist almost understates our sentiment on God's grace in our lives: "The boundary lines have fallen for me in pleasant places; surely

I have a delightful inheritance."[10] I like days when the overwhelming reflection of my heart is such.

But this story is equally a part of the biblical narrative. The gospel writer, Matthew, recounts the story when Jesus walked on a storm-tossed sea. Earlier, Jesus Himself told the disciples to go on ahead of Him. I am sure He was aware of the impending crisis they were to be thrust into; the disciples, however, were not.

Doing what Jesus told them to do was safe. After all, they were seasoned fishermen and experienced sailors; this lake was familiar territory. This was such an ordinary task, so they would not have given it a second thought. But in this ordinary, familiar moment, a storm blew up in the middle of the night, as storms often do, and they were caught unaware. Jesus, on the other hand, was still in the mountain elevations. He felt the wind blowing before they experienced the storm.

---

[10] Psalms 16:6 NIV

It reminds me of the anxiety Martha displayed when she said to Jesus, "If you had been here, my brother would not have died."[9] "If you had been here..." Those words echo across the generations still.

So why does God lead us into stormy seas? Why does He wait when people are dying? Why does He... This is where you fill in the blanks with your story. As much as I would like to reveal a great truth to answer such questions, the reality is I am still asking myself.

But what I do see is this fact: God knows, and He leads us into what we do not know. The apostle Peter puts it this way: "Dear friends, do not be surprised at the fiery ordeal that has come on you to test you, as though something strange were happening to you."[11]

Some experiences are strange things, indeed—random, unexpected, foreign, even

---

[11] 10 1 Peter 4:12 NIV

unnatural— something we have never encountered before. Jesus has foreknowledge, and we get blindsided.

The disciples were terrified and cried out in fear. The intensity of this moment is sobering. Seasoned and experienced fishermen became terrified by the environment they were accustomed to. This was not just a prank; these men assessed the end was near.

"Jesus has foreknowledge, and we get blindsided."

Fast forward to the outcome: They did not die; a totally new, never-seen-before miracle was revealed. God showed another level of His ability. And the disciples witnessed a side of God few have ever experienced.

So, yes, God does lead us into the worst-ever experiences, where we despair of life itself, to show us He walks on the storm which threatens us. Get this point: He walks on that which threatens us. Fear is confronted, stared down, but not by some brave warrior who is never intimidated.

Fear is confronted by ordinary people who are terrified, by those who wonder if they will see the next sunrise. And yet, they live to see another day. In the light of this new day, they know a God they did not know before.

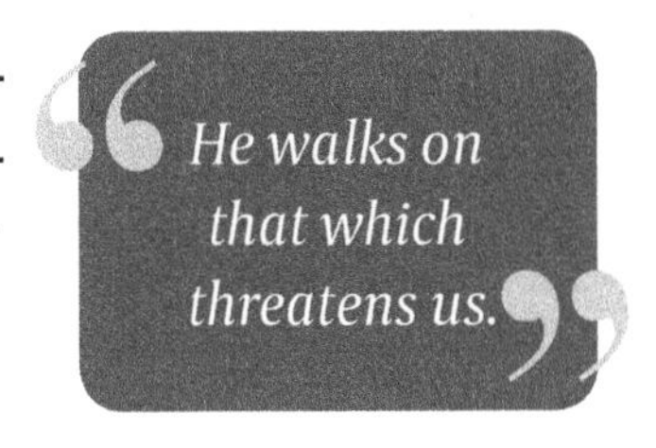

So, let's talk about fear for a moment. Courage is not the absence of fear but moving forward into the unknown. The outcome may be messy, and often is. Crisis is seldom neat and tidy; bravado is not showcased. There is no place to portray a cool hand Luke, or an iron-clad fearless heart. The reality is we are terrified, threatened, crying out in despair. Yet, the sunrise reveals us to be in the same boat with the One who walks on the storm. And, for a brief moment, you walked on the storm also.

So, here is the point. These disciples had known Jesus as a wonder-worker, but by the next morning, their understanding went to another level; "Truly you are the Son of God."[12] Here it is: Life's disappointments introduce us to a God we did not know before—mysterious, perhaps, but known at least in part.

[12] Matthew 14:33 NIV

Chapter 5
GOD CONCEALS

Not every mystery has to wait for eternity.

The book of Proverbs offers sagely wisdom, some of which raises as many questions as it answers. One such passage seems appropriate to our discussion. "It is the glory of God to conceal a matter; to search out a matter is the glory of kings."[13] Two things become apparent: God conceals some things, and those who search out such matters are assigned the glory of kings. Said another way, there is great reward for those who discover what is on the other side of life's mysteries.

Think of an arduous adventure, with the intent of discovering great treasure. The journey is difficult and not without hardship, perhaps even with

[13] Proverbs 25:2 NIV

losses along the way. However, once discovered, the treasure is so significant and valuable, difficulties experienced become insignificant.

Jesus Himself gave similar parables in Matthew, chapter thirteen, describing the value of finding the kingdom of God. There was a man who made a discovery in a field; so great was the find, he sold everything he had to purchase the field.

Then, there was a pearl merchant who discovered a pearl of great value. Again, he sold everything to make this one purchase. In both cases, the value of the discovery was believed to be so great that whatever the cost, it was a bargain too good to pass up.

May I suggest our lives are that journey, and some things we give up along the way are worth the treasure we discover? In fact, the greater the losses we have encountered, the greater is the treasure to be discovered.

If you can embrace this, it may help to reframe what has been taken from you, and rather let you see it as what you have given up in exchange to discover a bigger God. Nothing is ever lost when viewed from the perspective of giving a sacrifice.

But before straying too far from the Scripture, let's put this under the microscope: God conceals mysteries. I'm sure you would agree life's greatest secrets are seldom taught in a classroom. They are discovered on the journey of life, often at the expense of cuts, bruises, and scars. No one makes it to heaven without a few battle scars. But more on that later.

"Nothing is ever lost when viewed from the perspective of giving a sacrifice."

For now, perhaps you ask, "Why does God conceal Himself and His ways?" I could never venture an explanation of God's intentions. However, I suspect it has more to do with the limits of our understanding, as opposed to His willingness to be known.

Our faith is hijacked when the focus is on "how" and "when." We are better served if we can adopt the belief, "My God will deliver me"; the method is left to Him.

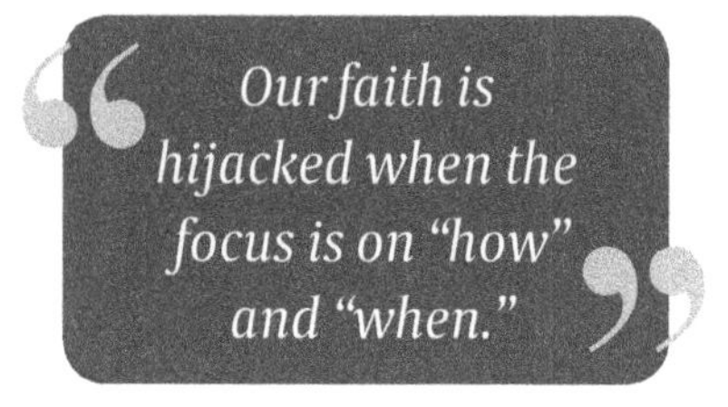

The book of Daniel, chapter three, tells the story of three men of unshakable faith: Shadrach, Meshach, and Abednego. When threatened to be thrown into a furnace of fire, their conviction of steel enabled them to take a stand in opposition to a godless despot. The essence of their protest is, Our God is able to deliver us from this furnace, but if He does not, we will not bow[14]. Their faith was not in the outcome; their faith was in God.

If we make resolution the goal, we short-circuit faith. What if resolution does not come? Is God any less God? A life of faith is not a formula; it

---

[14] Daniel 3: 16-18 NIV

is a relationship. God is not a principle; He is God. We diminish our understanding of who He is if we believe we understand all facets of His character. News flash: you will never know the full perspective of who God is. Our life is a pursuit of discovering this God of mystery. His purpose of developing character in us is a greater priority than overcoming a situation.

The English pastor and evangelist Allen Redpath made this statement, “The conversion of a soul is the miracle of a moment, but the manufacture of a saint is the task of a lifetime.”[15] Said another way, God has a higher purpose to develop His character in us than to make our character comfortable.

Let me get back to the thought of the journey to heaven. I want to be clear: Jesus paid the price for our entrance into heaven, and we add nothing to it. It is entirely by His grace, plus nothing. That being said, this journey, by the testimony of the Scripture, as well as the example of all who have

---

[15] https://www.christianquotes.info

gone before, would tell us no one gets through this life unscathed. Getting to heaven is not a parade for the pretty; it probably more closely resembles a movie in which relentless perseverance overcomes evil—bruised, bloody, and torn, but overcoming. Perhaps this overstates the matter. It may even risk the misconception that salvation comes by our own work and perseverance. Nothing could be further from the truth. But make no mistake; this journey of life takes us through more than a few minefields.

The apostle Paul prepared the leadership of the young and newly established churches in Asia Minor with these words:

> After they had preached the gospel to that city and had made many disciples, they returned to Lystra and to Iconium and to Antioch, strengthening the souls of the disciples, encouraging them to continue in the faith, and saying, "***Through***

> ***many tribulations we must enter the kingdom of God.***[16]

It hardly seems appropriate to encourage new recruits with, "***Through many tribulations we must enter the kingdom of God***." Our mindset of ease and comfort runs counter to any hint of hardship and endurance. While we may applaud the victory lap, we often overlook the pain and discipline of training which made the victory possible.

Don't get me wrong; I prefer and enjoy comfort and ease throughout the journey. But we fall into a trap to think all of life is that way and risk becoming disillusioned when it's not. This is compounded by misguided theologies, which leads us to think God will ensure our exemption from hardships in this life. The truth may very well be that God uses our disappointments to develop character and greater purpose.

---

[16] Acts 14:21-22 NASB

Our hardships may serve to make a wonderful introduction; you get to know yourself, and you get to know a dimension of God's character, which is unknowable in the shallow waters of personal preservation.

Then Jesus said to His disciples,

> If anyone wishes to come after Me, he must deny himself, and take up his cross and follow Me. For whoever wishes to save his life will lose it; but whoever loses his life for My sake will find it. For what will it profit a man if he gains the whole world and forfeits his soul? Or what will a man give in exchange for his soul?[17]

Those words burned in the heart of the young seminarian Jim Elliot, who penned the following in his diary: "He is no fool who gives what he cannot keep, to gain what he cannot lose."[18] Jim Elliot

---

[17] Matthew 6:24-26 NIV

[18] Journal excerpt from *Shadow of the Almighty* (1989) by Elisabeth Elliot, Jim Elliot, 1949

was one of five missionaries who were credited as having taken the gospel to a totally primitive culture, but not without great sacrifice.

One might correctly conclude that a life well lived is not necessarily pampered, but rather spent, battered by a few storms, proven, and matured.

But let's keep it real. Simply encountering loss is not a guaranteed path to maturity. Adversity has the potential to create casualties. The body count of those whose devastations ruined them to future productivity is high. You may know a few names on that list, but your name does not need to be one of them.

All too often, people may be so attached to a past moment that they remain at the station; all the while, that train has left. Bewilderment morphs into a life of its own. Stagnation is not a way of life, and anything that grows in a stagnated situation is not good or desirable.

Our energy is better spent managing unwelcomed change, rather than losing heart over past moments. Your Shepherd has not abandoned you; He is leading you to the path with your name on it— the one marked out for you. The treasure of discovering purpose knows no sacrifice too great.

Exiting a familiar path is not for the faint of heart. The psalmist admonishes us, "Be of good courage, and he shall strengthen your heart, all ye that hope in the LORD."[19] God will strengthen your heart. You are not without resource, although you may be starting again at zero. The reset button has been pushed, and what God has in mind for you will exceed your expectations.

---

[19] Psalm 31:24 KJV

Chapter 6
A Dark Place

Dark places in life are transitional.
Hardships introduce new understanding.

Psalm 23 is often quoted at funerals, but it truly reveals more about how to live than how to die. Here, you will find one of those worst-ever experiences. "Even though I walk through the darkest valley, I will fear no evil, for you are with me; your rod and your staff, they comfort me."[20] There is a darkness so penetrating and absolute it is referred to as the "valley of the shadow of death." More than just a darkness over our eyes, it is felt within. It can be disorientating, confusing, and pervasive to the point of paralysis. Next steps are unknown and uncertain. Sheep fear such a narrow, confining canyon to pass through, as do we.

---

[20] Psalm 23:4 NIV

Sheep could never imagine their shepherd leading them into such places, and we think Jesus would never take us into such a region of darkness. This is not so much a place of evil intent, although the evil one is not far away in those places, ready to take advantage of our disorientation and confusion. Do not underestimate just how bleak and alarming the dark places can be. Rarely, if ever, will good decisions be made from a heart of fear. How often we regret decisions made during the dark periods in our lives.

Let me show you a moment from the life of the apostle Peter. I think you would agree that he had experienced more than a few miracle moments in his time with Jesus. He walked in the steps few have ever experienced. He was not a spiritual lightweight; yet, this is the same man who, in one night, betrayed his Lord, his friend, and himself. So profound was his denial of Jesus, not once, not twice, but three times. How could such a significant person of faith fail so badly? How many times have we asked that question?

Peter was not spiritually bipolar. He cannot be dismissed as one who was weak or a novice. Even the mighty walk through dark places.

Isaiah the prophet puts it this way:

> Even youths grow tired and weary,
> and young men stumble and fall;
> but those who hope in the Lord
> will renew their strength.
> They will soar on wings like eagles;
> they will run and not grow weary,
> they will walk and not be faint.[21]

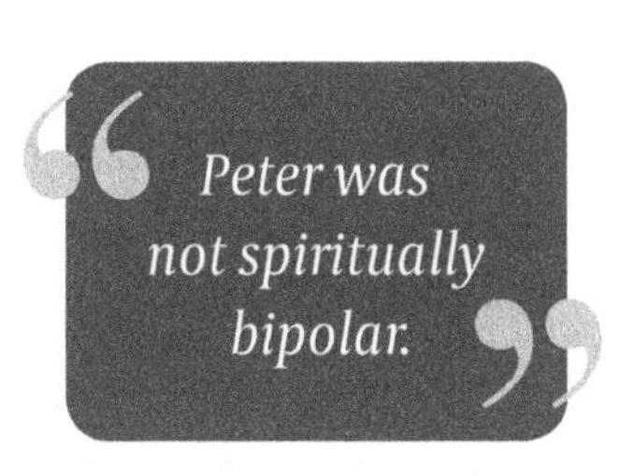

Similar to the night on the lake when a storm threatened the disciples' lives, Jesus rescued Peter from drowning in despair. This was the same storm where Peter, for a brief moment, walked where Jesus walked—on stormy waters. Jesus knew the

[21] Isaiah 40:31-32 NIV

outcome then, and He knows the outcome of the storm in your life now.

Jesus said to Peter:

> Simon, Simon, behold, Satan demanded to have you, that he might sift you like wheat, but I have prayed for you that your faith may not fail. And when you have turned again, strengthen your brothers.[22]

Jesus saw beyond Peter's dark valley, as He does with us. The Shepherd knows the valley of darkness is a place of transition to arrive in green pastures. That place of darkness we encounter is for a moment, and it is a moment in which Jesus Himself prays our faith will not fail; and that we would be strengthened to help others. And so emerging from the dark shadows comes an empowered one—one who was once too weak to hardly care for him/herself, yet now is able to provide care to fellow sojourners.

---

[22] Luke 22:31-32 ESV

Many are the lessons gleaned along the journey. Weakness gives way to strength, albeit gradually, perhaps. Priorities change; relationships are embraced differently. There is a new appreciation for the beauty of the moment and a deeper understanding of who God is. We also gain a clearer perspective of who we are.

Chapter 7

DOES GOD REPEAT HIMSELF?

Why do we attempt to shrink God to the limits of our understanding?

Ever wonder if God repeats Himself? Have there ever been two miracles exactly the same? Do you think He has exhausted His creative abilities? So, if something has never been done before, I wonder if that does not excite His creative juices just a bit? Could it be our praying formulates a plan of action rooted in past experience? If so, do we limit the Almighty?

Perhaps when praying, we should leave the door open for God to answer in a way we have never considered. And when He answers your prayer, can you recognize it?

We view history from a smug filter of hindsight. The Pharisees and scribes were the educated and studied intelligentsia of the day, whose primary role was to look for the Messiah. Jesus was born and grew up amongst them, but their beliefs and filters would not allow them to see the very one they were looking for.

We scoff at their religious blindness, but if God shows up in our lives differently than we have anticipated, I wonder if our perception would be any better. Jesus alluded to this when He said:

> For I was hungry and you gave me nothing to eat, I was thirsty and you gave me nothing to drink, I was a stranger and you did not invite me in, I needed clothes and you did not clothe me, I was sick and in prison and you did not look after me.[23]

Without question, Jesus was teaching us to see Him in the overlooked and forgotten. But more

---

[23] Matthew 25:41-44 NIV

fundamentally, He indicated His appearance may be different than what we anticipated. After all, who ever heard of a king being born in a stable?

God delights in confounding the wisdom of the expected and enjoys the simplicity of the child to accomplish His objectives. So, how could we possibly anticipate God's next move? The limits of our understanding distort and mask our views. How foolish to attempt to comprehend and explain an infinite God through the filter of our past experiences?

"How foolish to attempt to comprehend and explain an infinite God through the filter of our past experiences?"

Setbacks we encounter do not define us. At best, they are a comma in the stories of our lives, not a period. The Author of our faith is writing a marvelous mystery book, and you are playing a leading role.

Chapter 8
TOXICITY

Certain people and situations
are like a good diet—
we become better people
by avoiding a few things.

Toxicity, by definition, is a specific degree of being toxic or poisonous. While it makes a great murder mystery when the character is poisoned deviously and intentionally, but in real life, we need to avoid toxins at all cost.

Some situations—and may I even say, some people who wander into our lives—can be toxic. Now, if that sounds too cruel, allow me to expound. They may not be of a sinister nature plotting our demise, but when mixed with the composition of our personalities, experiences, and filters—or lack of—well, let's just say, it is a blending of compounds that should not be combined.

Could it be that the path we have been on is not really the one marked out for us? Or maybe, a better understanding might be, perhaps we are not the right person for that path. I suspect we have transitions to go through to become the better person who is within.

Allow me to suggest that, all too often, we have a naive view of things in our lives. We simply do not recognize poisonous and hostile environments. Certain situations may be toxic to the accomplishment of God's intended purpose.

Again, the writer of the book of Hebrews offers insight about transitioning to the path marked out for us.

> No discipline seems pleasant at the time, but painful. Later on, however, it produces

> a harvest of righteousness and peace ***for those who have been trained by it***.[24]

The discipline spoken of here is not correction for wrong behavior. Rather, it has more to do with the discipline of training which an athlete undergoes in preparation of an event. This statement from Scripture is entirely in the context of running a race marked out for us. In fact, verse seven states it emphatically: "Endure hardship as discipline." All of life is training.

And notice the reward: "*and peace for those who have been trained by it*." For those whose hearts are embroiled in conflict and turmoil, the reward of peace is an oasis on the journey.

This is not self-help talk, elevating you to be a better you. More to the point, it is reframing to view all of life from God's vantage point. Difficulties we encounter train us to understand God is shaping us. Purpose is secondary; primary to purpose

---

[24] Hebrews 12:11 NIV

is character. To fulfill destiny, we must first of all become the right person.

The apostle Paul gives a clear example of this when he writes:

> Brothers and sisters, I do not consider myself yet to have taken hold of it. But one thing I do: Forgetting what is behind and straining toward what is ahead, I press on toward the goal to win the prize for which God has called me heavenward in Christ Jesus.[25]

You cannot embrace the future while holding tight to the past. Letting go of the past does not mean erasing our memory banks. Past memories constitute a large part of who we are today. But we discover a problem when we try to recreate the past and relive it. As good as previous times have been, they are not roadmaps for our future. Your

[25] Philippians 3:13-14 NIV

life was never designed to become a museum; reenacting history is best left to historians.

I wonder if the reason some people tend to live in the past is that the present has become too difficult. It is more comfortable to let our minds go back to an easier time, when things were less complicated. But have you ever noticed how reflections of the good old days sanitize our memory and omit the difficult aspects of those times?

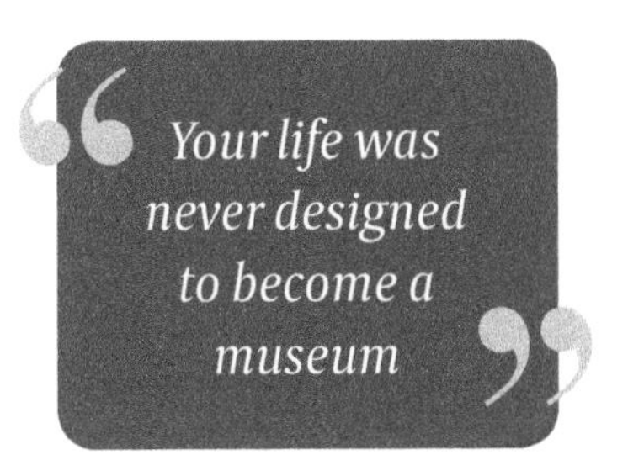

Chapter 9

A HIGHER VANTAGE POINT

On the other side of disappointment,
we gain a perspective of purpose.

The Bible is full of examples from which you and I can learn. Consider a personality we find in the pages of the Old Testament, Joseph. His story spans several chapters of Genesis, beginning in chapter thirty through to the end of the book. Most of his early life was unfair. Let's inventory a few dynamics of this young man's home life. His mother died prematurely. He grew up in a blended family, where his brothers held great animosity against him. Compounded to this, his father, Jacob, did not hide the special gifts and favor he conveyed on Joseph. This only inflamed the outright hatred of his brothers. They wanted to murder him, but instead compromised and agreed to sell him into slavery[26].

Dysfunctional families are not a new dynamic to our generation. Although God was at work in Joseph's life, dysfunction was very much a part of his home life. Such a contrast.

At an approximate age of seventeen, Joseph found himself in a foreign country, not knowing the language or customs, and all his rights were reduced to those of a slave. After years of faithful service, he was falsely accused of rape[27]. If life as a slave was not bad enough, his new reality became the confines of prison. After years of compliance to prison life, he was betrayed by a fellow inmate, resulting in denial of release from prison.

The years spanning from early childhood to adulthood were marked by adversity, misrepresentation, and failed relationships. Although not stated

---

[26] Genesis 37:12-28 NIV

[27] Genesis 39:6-20 NIV

in Scripture, I suspect there were many sleepless nights when he wondered, *Why me, and how could life be so unfair?*

However, to understand Joseph, one must comprehend an underlying motivation in his life. Joseph knew something about destiny and a sense of purpose. Despite the mistreatment of family and others, he knew God had a path marked out for him. So strong was this drive, it spanned across cultures and decades.

The point to make here is that Joseph had to grow into his purpose. Although he knew God had a plan, he wasn't yet the person equipped for the role. A case could be made that many of his problems were actually self-imposed, due to immaturity in knowing how to express his motivation.

Maybe this is where you relate to Joseph's life. Some situations and experiences have been aggravated because of what you felt inside. Compromise wasn't an option, and isolation became the result. Words got in the way of intentions, sabotaging motivations. Had you been given an opportunity for a do-over, the outcome could have been different. But all too often, second chances simply don't come around.

In hindsight, it is now apparent you were not yet ready. Hence the role of adversity: our challenges transform us into the person prepared for the race marked out for us. Disappointment, betrayal, and losses all discipline or train you for the unique role for which God has specifically created you.

In Joseph's life, the influence of his ultimate role was generational. The impact of your life may not be recorded in history's pages, but nonetheless, the impact you have on others can be dramatic.

It was only later in life that Joseph had the perspective of an elevated view. Rather than words of revenge, he saw purpose. "You intended to harm me, but God intended it for good to accomplish what is now being done, the saving of many lives."[28] Joseph was able to look beyond his brothers, who were the cause of an avalanche of adversity; he could see there was a destiny to be fulfilled; another path to be walked upon, and he had been groomed to be that person.

To those who have been marginalized by adversaries, Joseph would tell us that while others meant destruction, God has a higher agenda, a different path. When passed by and set aside, understand God has the final say. Your validation and vindication come from Him at an appointed time.

The book of James gives this instruction: "And let endurance have its ***perfect result,*** so that you may be perfect and ***complete***, ***lacking in nothing***."[29] See these words: ***perfect result***, ***complete***, ***lacking nothing***. We become changed people, better people—trained to fulfill the roles God has mapped out for us.

---

[28] Genesis 50:20 NIV

[29] James 1:4 NIV

The song in your heart may have gone silent for a time, but you can regain your voice to speak with authority in specific situations. Your adversity is not in vain. Recognition may not necessarily be the stamp of validation. Your experiences empower you to speak with authority in situations where others are mute.

> *"Your experiences empower you to speak with authority in situations where others are mute"*

So, could it be that you are being groomed for a role you have not yet seen? Our most important moments in life may not be associated with a job description or title. When viewed from the perspective of eternity, the influence we have on people will be our greatest legacy.

Chapter 10
TRANSFORMED PEOPLE

The progress we make in our spiritual life does not elevate us above our humanity.

The apostle Peter was indeed a transformed person. I so appreciate the honesty of the Scriptures to show how God works with flawed people. Earlier, we saw Peter at perhaps the lowest moment of his life; so overwhelmingly caving into the pressure of a servant girl, denying any knowledge of his Lord and friend, Jesus.

Many would find the magnitude of such an epic embarrassment too great to overcome. But I want you to see this same man standing before a crowd of 3,000, fearlessly acknowledging the same Jesus he had previously denied. Yes, he was empowered by the Spirit of God, but there is also an inner confidence, which was the result of working through fears and failures.

His future role left no room for past insecurities. Peter had to experience the weakness of his inner fears firsthand before he could boldly serve in the role of an early church father.

The author of the epistle is a different man than he was on his first day as a disciple. Being called by Jesus was the beginning of Peter's journey of transformation. Mistakenly, we might imagine that being called out by Jesus to become a chosen disciple would be the moment of a lifetime. But instead of the pinnacle, this was just the beginning. Little did Peter know where the journey would take him.

You may look at the future with bewilderment, and perhaps even fear. But the promise of the Scripture is, "For we are God's masterpiece. He has created us anew in Christ Jesus, so we can do the good things he planned for us long ago."[30]

For those who have felt diminished in life, dismissed by others, and reduced to self-doubt, realize you are a masterpiece, of which God Himself is the craftsman. Your current situation is a transition, not a conclusion. God's plan continues to unfold in the midst of this moment.

We simply cannot afford to let the embarrassment of past failures or the victory of past successes tether our feet to an old path. The journey into a new day requires vision for what lies ahead. Distracted driving will always lead to trouble.

Labels, titles, and awards are all wonderful. They make great conversation when displayed openly, but rarely are inner victories recognized. And yet such are the building materials the Lord looks for in transforming you for future roles. The Lord builds people, not institutions.

---

[30] Ephesians 2:10 NLT

It is such a great study to examine how Jesus referred to Peter. In John 1:42, Jesus called Peter Cephas, an Aramaic name meaning "rock."[31] But in Matthew 16, Jesus made reference to Peter as the foundation of the church. There are many opinions on this passage, but this man who was once hard like a stone became molded into the person Jesus could use.

So, whether you see yourself in the life of Peter or not, here is one thing I know: your capacity for change knows no limits. God is working His grace on your behalf. Paul writes to the Philippian church these words: "And I am certain that God, who began the good work within you, will continue his work until it is finally finished on the day when Christ Jesus returns."[32]

The relentless Creator will never cease His work of molding you into the person who leaves an impact on this world. Broken as you may be, God

---

[31] www.biblestudytools.com/dictionary/peter/

[32] Philippians 1:6 NLT

is not. And He will use your brokenness to accomplish His objectives in you and through you.

Actually, being wounded and broken is what God looks for. "The Lord is close to the brokenhearted and saves those who are crushed in spirit."[33] You may feel God is nowhere in sight. While others may have abandoned you, rest assured—He is close.

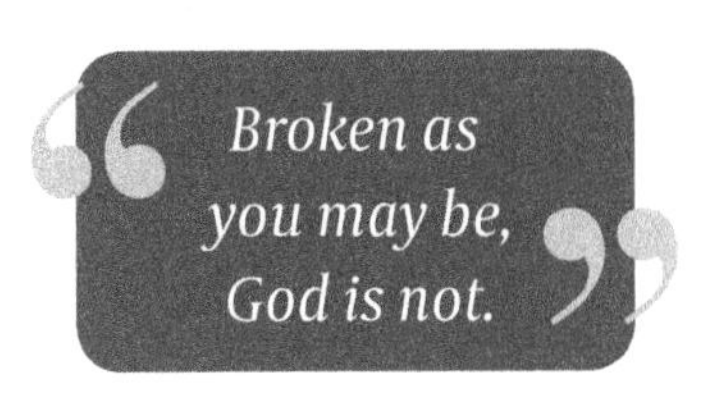

[33] Psalms 34:18 NIV

Chapter 11
CAN YOU IMAGINE?

Trading the known for what
God holds in store
now, that is a walk of faith.

Do you think that you have a better imagination than God? Consider what the apostle Paul wrote:

> Things which eye has not seen and ear has not heard, and *which* have not entered the heart of man, all that God has prepared for those who love Him.[34]

So, our Lord has things in mind for us which we have not even thought of or dared to imagine. How scary and exciting is that?

---

[34] 1 Corinthians 2:9 NASB

Rather than clinging to the past and what was, can you dare to believe God has something greater in mind for you? He has plans which, to this point, you have never thought of. Have you ever said, "If you told me a year ago that I would be doing this..."?

I have to wonder if the familiar life we have molded for ourselves may resemble a rut. And after all, the only difference between a rut and a grave is the size. Now, some ruts can be comfortable; not so much because it suits our needs, but because it is known. And we like known.

A job maybe killing you a minute at a time. Creativity drains away with each passing day.

Certain relationships may be taking a toll on you; others see it, but somehow you are impervious to how it diminishes you.

An addiction satisfies a need, but in reality, it is killing you. While you may want change, the trap has been set, and you are caught.

The book of Psalms presents this picture: "Surely he will save you from the fowler's snare and from the deadly pestilence."[35] The nature of a trap is that it does not look like a trap. It seems appropriate; it meets a need; it is good enough. This is the deception of bait.

But good enough never is. May I suggest that anything which entangles and sidetracks us to a different path other than the one marked out for us just might be a trap? Your best creative self is shackled, entrapped, surviving, but not enjoying. You would love just a moment to catch a deep breath of air from a higher elevation, but you cannot. You are stuck.

So, why the reluctance of letting go? Well, it is familiar, known, and comfortable. You draw your identity by describing your family, your job, your address. You are what you do. You are the people around you. You are what you possess.

---

[35] Psalm 91:3 NIV

Perhaps just seeing those words on paper helps you realize what a shallow and superficial understanding of life this is. We are more than the number of likes on social media. Titles do not define you. You were created by God; not self-made, not made by the image and recognition of others. We are not products of our culture. Rather, we were created to reflect the enormous nature and grace of an infinitely creative God.

I have to wonder at times; is God's nature veiled because I prefer to stay in my rut, instead of believing He might want better for me? I need to shake off the familiar, the comfortable, and the known to become all He imagined I could be through Him.

We become so conditioned to our rut; we focus on making it more comfortable. God, on the other hand, has an agenda of imploding our rut. He sees what we cannot. The rut is a trap, and your freedom is lost. Life continues in confinement but is hardly enjoyed; existence, but not living.

In fact, maybe we should align our praying with God's agenda. Discovering the person you have been created to be needs to start with understanding the deficit in your life. More than the circumstances changing, this discovery must begin with you. It may not be just an adjustment you need; tweaking the rut is probably not the fix.

> *After all, a nice trap is still a trap.*

Can you abandon what you have been working hard to create in order to become the person you have never been? Remember the admonishment from Hebrews 12: "Throw off ***everything*** that hinders." After all, a nice trap is still a trap.

Chapter 12
THE CAVE

In moments of pain, you find
others who are also hurting.
Healing comes as we help each other.

Isolation changes people. Most times, solitary confinement is seen as a punishment to correct misbehavior. When everything is stripped away, and all that is left is you, you take assessment of your life. It can break or make the strongest of character. As horrific as being a prisoner of war would be, there are heroic accounts of those who discovered an undeniable spirit of courage and strength.

Isolation can develop a deeper level of character in us. Immediately after his encounter with Jesus, Paul sought isolation in the Arabian desert for a period of three years[36]. He needed solitude to rethink the direction to which he had given himself. Can you imagine what it must have been like to realize everything you had learned and stood for was wrong? Just think how much unwinding needed to take place in his mind and spirit to recognize Jesus as Messiah. This is the same Jesus whom Paul had strategically positioned his entire life to discredit.

It is more than a bit ironic that this angry and prideful man had to be knocked to the ground to come to his senses. Being wrong can be tough.

Let's consider another who had to cry "uncle." Jonah, a prophet from the Old Testament, was filled with hatred for the people whom God loved. When given the opportunity to change the direction of an entire culture, he chose to go the other way[37]. Yet, God is relentless to bring about a better man in His called one. Accordingly, He planned an

---

[36] Galatians 1:17-18 NIV

[37] Jonah 1:3 NLT

extraordinary intervention, which involved a very large fish.

And even after Jonah had reconsidered his position, his attitude revealed a residue of past prejudice and bias. He wallowed in depression because his expectations were not met. God had the audacity to do the unimaginable and go against Jonah's misguided emotions.

The book of Jonah finishes with perhaps one of the most poignant scriptures of the Bible: "But Nineveh has more than 120,000 people living in spiritual darkness … ***Shouldn't I feel sorry for such a great city***?"[38] I wonder if God does not say that about the megacities of our world today. He looks for those who can believe there is a higher purpose than shallow preferences. He is looking for those who will become uncomfortable with their comfortable.

Then there was David. Although he was selected to be God's person of choice, we find him running and

[38] Jonah 4:11 NLT

hiding to save his life. His hunt for isolation took him to a dark cave, the Cave of Adullam[39]. Have you been there?

> *Have you noticed that in your painful moments, when you just want to be left alone, you encounter others who are hurting as well?*

Wanting to be alone and hide away from visibility, David found anything but. In fact, four hundred others were seeking refuge as well. Have you noticed that in your painful moments, when you just want to be left alone, you encounter others who are hurting as well?

These cave-dwellers were distressed, in debt, and discontent. If David's problems were not enough, he ran into others just like him. There seems to be no shortage of distraught people wanting things to be different. We are given a choice: blend in and become one of the many, or see God's providence.

---

[39] 1 Samuel 22:1-3 NIV

We observe a dynamic of leadership in David's life. Regardless of how limiting circumstances may be, when leadership is the DNA of a person, leaders surface. So, David began to train his new disgruntled associates. Later, they became known as David's mighty men, leaving a legacy of exploits.

David went to the cave with one plan; God had another. He wanted to disappear; God wanted someone to invest in the disenfranchised of his day.

Who occupies your cave with you? Pain may have you so incapacitated, you can barely plot direction for the next day. How in the world could God ask you to give direction to others? While your situation may seem random, He directed your steps to this cave. What you have learned in this journey can indeed help others who are a step or two behind. But make no mistake; there are others in this cave with you, and your experience can leave a well of water to refresh others.

Chapter 13

A New Current

Discovery of purpose comes
as a result of learning who you are.

Our lives are not random; God is continually establishing His purpose in us. The adversity we encounter is not in vain. Here is a powerful promise:

> "In the same way I will not cause pain without allowing ***something new to be born***."[40]

So, could it be that there is purpose in our pain? Can you believe your brokenness brings new birth?

New thing to be born... I can almost hear the scoffing. But may I remind you of Abraham's wife,

---

[40] Isaiah 66:9 NCV

Sarah? She laughed at the promise of her dream of having a son, because of her old age.

No situation is beyond transformation. Age is not a limiting factor. Passage of time does not dwarf God's agenda. It is never too late, too far gone, or too distant for the Joseph in you to be revealed.

After experiencing setbacks and disappointments, fatigue often is prominent. The idea of anything new is just simply too exhausting. However, new birth inherently brings renewed energy.

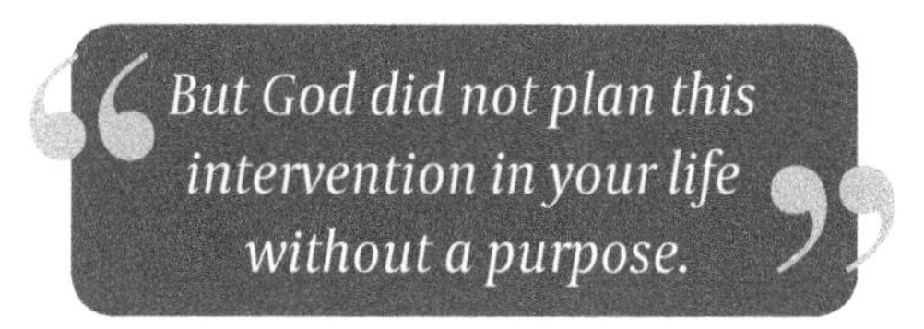

Something new is born out of our pain. Just what that something is may be ambiguous at first. We ask, "What good could possibly come of this?" But God did not plan this intervention in your life without a purpose.

Let me add that not all interventions are successful. Patterns can be so entrenched that change is pushed away and not welcomed, but some will see a way to move on. The crisis you face presents the opportunity for change. Actually, it may demand change.

The Westminster Catechism was a document written by the early church leaders in a question-and-answer format summarizing the beliefs of the Christian faith. The question is asked, which is still relevant for you and I, "What is the chief end of man?" To which the answer follows, "I believe man's chief end is to glorify God, and to enjoy Him forever.[41]" Is it possible that the great reward for the transformed person is to enjoy God more, and in doing so, bring glory to Him?

All of life is a process to correct our vision to see the God who loves us, to enjoy Him, and to learn the art of authentic worship. For some, knowing God, enjoying Him, and worshiping Him may not seem to be enough. Perhaps this is a clue that

---

41 www.shortercatechism.com

the work of transformation has not finished its perfecting work for those individuals.

We need to develop a matrix perspective on how we view life. There is the here and now, but there is also life in eternity. A vision toward the greatest part of our lives can shape how we handle the disappointments we face today.

Perhaps the validation we look for is recognition in the eyes of our peers. But in reality, I suspect that, that will be a shallow victory. Happier is the person validated by God, who lives with the smile of His approval. True contentment empowers, and in the updraft of the quieted soul, we find a new strength. Take a closer look at the following passage from the Scriptures.

> Do you not know?
> Have you not heard?
> The Lord is the everlasting God,
> the Creator of the ends of the earth.
> He will not grow tired or weary,
> and his understanding no one can fathom.

> He gives strength to the weary
> and increases the power of the weak.
> Even youths grow tired and weary,
> and young men stumble and fall;
> but those who hope in the Lord
> will renew their strength.
> They will soar on wings like eagles;
> they will run and not grow weary,
> they will walk and not be faint.[42]

So, when we grow weary, God does not. When we can walk away from the fight for self-acclamation, we begin to catch the current of His strength. Life lived without the stress of being our own architect and engineer is life enjoyed.

After all, could it be that the happiness and contentment we so desperately run after is not so far from God's objective as well? For those who know their God and enjoy Him daily understand contentment.

---

[42] Isaiah 40:28-31 NIV

We strive to preserve and defend our path, not realizing how flawed it may be. Initially, the path we choose varies just one or two degrees from God's design. We would defend the difference as trivial and harmless. At first, the variance would seem negligible. But projected over a lifetime, we find ourselves a universe away from God's intention.

So, He interferes with our plans; He nudges us off course. He takes us down paths we would think unimaginable. Everything within us cries, "God, how could You!" Well, let's just call it a midcourse correction—an intervention which uncovers a truer purpose and fulfillment. You become tuned into the frequency you were designed to receive; static interference is gone.

Purpose is finally discovered—purpose not defined by title and accomplishments. Rather, this purpose is discovered in being, not in doing.

And see this paradox: the one who soars on eagle's wings does not accomplish less. Rather, the accomplishments have a different scale of measure. They might have more to do with investment in people than in portfolios.

It has been correctly stated that in our last moments, our reflections will not be on wishing we had spent more time at the office. Priorities become clear in that moment, and life is measured in terms of relationships, not accomplishments. Perhaps wisdom would tell us to orientate our lives with that compass today.

I would like to leave you with one final thought. Psalm 90:12 offers a life-changing prayer: "Teach us to number our days aright, that we may gain a heart of wisdom."[43] If we could only view the time-sensitive shelf life of our existence, and process each and every event from the vantage point of gaining a heart of wisdom, I believe we could see God's bigger purpose. The psalmist's prayer is, "Teach us," so apparently this is something we need to learn. It is not inherent, but rather a skill to be acquired.

---

[43] Psalm 90:12 NIV

You have a Heavenly Father who is ever crafting you to be more like Him and less like an imperfect image you have understood and pursued. My sincere prayer is that you will discover God's higher intent in the pain of your brokenness and disappointments.

On the other side of disappointment awaits an introduction. You will be introduced to a deeper, truer you, who discovers the richness of God's creation in you. And you will come to know a God who spares no expense to bring out the best in you.